A JOURNAL OF MEMORIES

Mom, For All Of Eternity

---

21 Time Capsules
to Keep Forever

Preserving moments that matter

*What we remember becomes
who we are.*

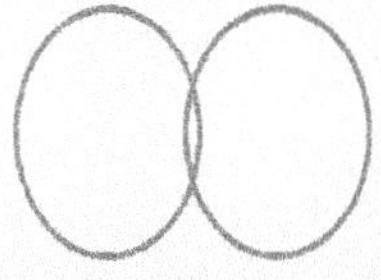

For all of eternity

Why This Book Exists

Life moves quickly. Moments that feel monumental fade into memory, and memories soften with time. This book exists to freeze moments in time before they slip away.

These 21 time capsules are more than prompts—they're an invitation to pause and reflect on the moments, people, and truths that have shaped who you are. They're a way to hold onto the extraordinary hidden within the ordinary.

In filling these pages, you're creating something precious: a record of your heart, your journey, and your wisdom. A gift for those you love—so they can truly know you, understand your story, and cherish the moments that mattered most.

This is your legacy. These are your truths. Preserved for all of eternity.

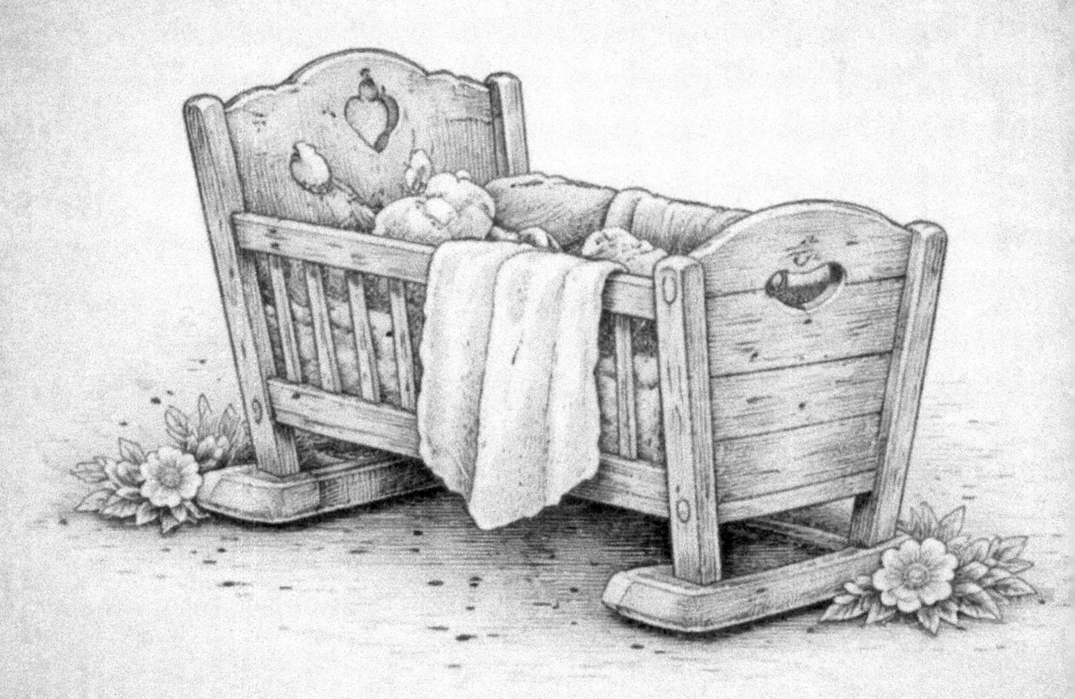

How This Book Works

Each page is a time capsule.

Open to one. Fill it when the moment feels right.

Date it. Seal it with your truth.

Then close the book.

This isn't meant to be read all at once.

Some pages are for today.

Some are meant for later.

Some for much, much later.

This book is meant to live with you—

not be rushed, not be finished.

Let it unfold slowly, one truth at a time.

This Time Capsule Belongs To

Given to by

Date received

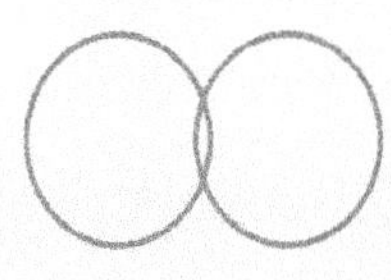

For all of eternity

#1

Sealed on: _______________

A truth I learned from you that I want to preserve forever is...

For all of eternity.

#2

Sealed on: _______________

A special memory with my mom
I've cherished is...

For all of eternity.

#3

Sealed on: ___________________

The moment I realized you were my hero...

For all of eternity.

#4

Sealed on: ______________________

The bravest thing I ever saw you do was...

For all of eternity.

*Love lives on
in what we choose to remember.*

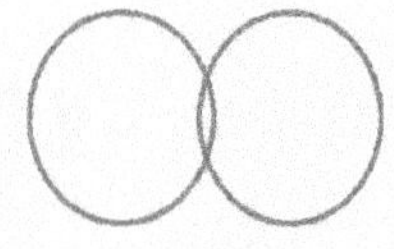

For all of eternity

#5

Sealed on: ___________________

A dream that still calls to me is...

For all of eternity.

#6

Sealed on: ___________________

The lesson that transformed everything for me...

For all of eternity.

#7

Sealed on: ___________________

A place that will forever hold a piece of my heart...

For all of eternity.

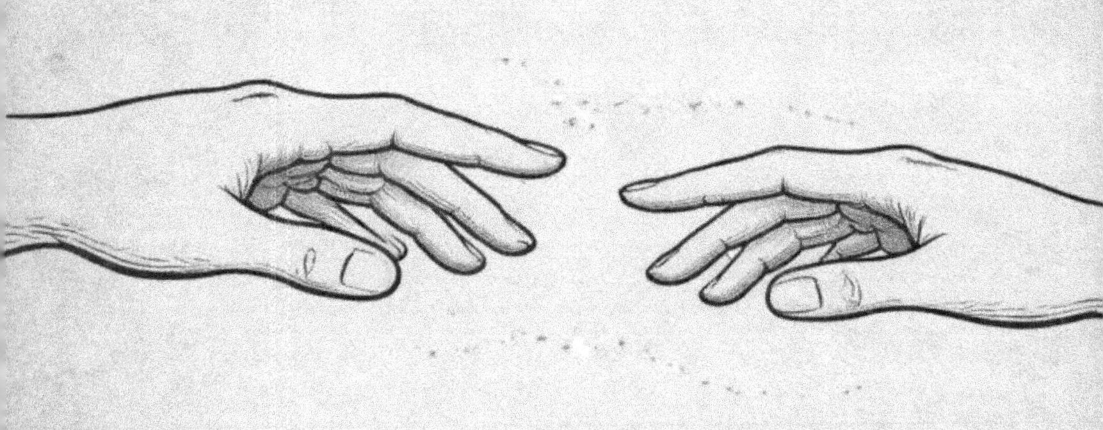

#8

Sealed on: ___________________

The time you supported me through a hard time was...

For all of eternity.

#9

Sealed on: _______________

What I want my kids to know about you is...

For all of eternity.

The heart remembers
what the mind forgets.

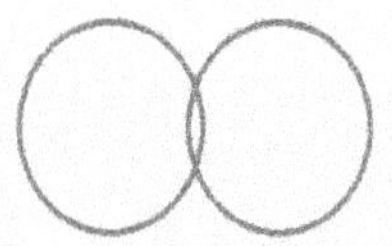

For all of eternity

#10

Sealed on: ___________________

How your love shaped me most deeply...

For all of eternity.

#11

Sealed on: _______________________

A belief I'll carry with me always...

For all of eternity.

#12

Sealed on: _______________

The day everything changed was when...

For all of eternity.

#13

Sealed on: _______________

Something beautiful I witnessed that no one else saw...

For all of eternity.

#14

Sealed on: _______________

A promise that I made with you that I kept...

For all of eternity.

These moments, these words—
they are your forever.

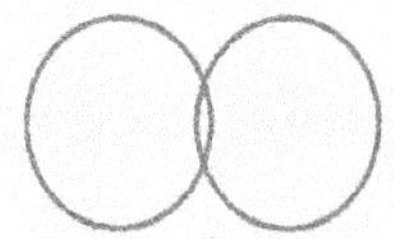

For all of eternity

#15

Sealed on: ___________________

The greatest gift you gave me was...

For all of eternity.

#16

Sealed on: _______________________

A joy I hope to never forget is...

For all of eternity.

#17

____

Sealed on: ____________________

What I've learned about resilience is...

#18

Sealed on: ___________________

The conversation that altered my perspective forever...

For all of eternity.

Mom

#19

Sealed on: ______________________

A moment of grace I experienced was...

For all of eternity.

In preserving our stories,
we honor our truth.

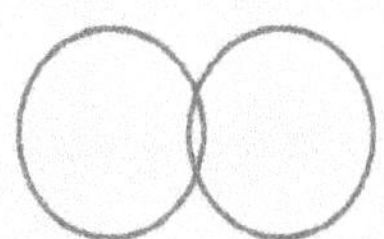

For all of eternity

#20

Sealed on: ______________________

The values I hope live on through you...

For all of eternity.

#21

Sealed on: ___________________

If I could preserve one feeling forever, it would be...

For all of eternity.

————————————————

Your truths are now preserved.

These pages hold the moments that shaped you,
the love that sustained you,
and the wisdom you've gathered along the way.

What you've written here will outlive the days,
the years, the seasons of your life.

This is your legacy.
These are your truths.

Sealed forever.

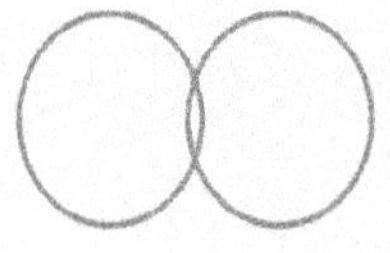

For all of eternity

www.ingramcontent.com/pod-product-compliance
Lightning Source LLC
Chambersburg PA
CBHW050046040726
47599CB00015B/1818